C000050931

IMAGES OF ENGLAND

WETHERBY
AND SURROUNDING VILLAGES

WETHERBY HISTORICAL TRUST

The History Press

First published in 2006 by Tempus Publishing Limited

Reprinted in 2011 by
The History Press
The Mill, Brimscombe Port,
Stroud, Gloucestershire, GL5 2QG
www.thehistorypress.co.uk

British Library Cataloguing in Publication Data.
A catalogue record for this book is available from the British Library.

ISBN 978 0 7524 4078 1

Series design and typesetting by Liz Rudderham.
Origination by Tempus Publishing Limited.
Printed in Great Britain.

Contents

Acknowledgements

The Wetherby Historical Trust wishes to acknowledge the contribution of its chairman, Dr J.S.H. Lodge, who has supplied a large number of these photographs from his personal collection. His knowledge of history, Wetherby, and the history of Wetherby has been invaluable in the compilation and documentation of this book.

The Trust would also like to acknowledge and thank the following, who have all supplied material for use in the book: Mr and Mrs M. Kay, Mr E. Kitchen, Miss I. Greaves, Mr E. Pope, *The Wetherby News,* the Wetherby Festival Committee, Wetherby in Bloom, The Wetherby Drama Society, the Wetherby Lions and Riding for the Disabled.

Introduction

A previous book of old photographs of Wetherby in this series compiled by Wetherby and District Historical Society was very well received. Subsequently more photographs have come to light presenting the opportunity to publish not only a further selection on Wetherby but also to include a dozen or so of the surrounding villages for which it was the market town and which are such an integral part of the district.

Wetherby has developed as the focal point for the area since at least 1240 when the Knights Templar obtained a Market Charter for the town. This role was enhanced in 1897 with the creation of the Wetherby Rural District Council which became responsible for the provision of housing, planning and matters of public health. These administrative functions were lost when local government reorganisation in 1974 split the rural district between Leeds Metropolitan City Council and the Harrogate District of the North Yorkshire County Council. Wetherby itself became a part of Leeds; a small fish in a very large pond. Also the great increase in car ownership has meant that many people in the villages now travel to Leeds, Harrogate and York for things that previously they would have obtained in Wetherby but none the less Wetherby and these villages still form a recognisable unit.

Inevitably the pictures gathered here are graphic illustrations of how these places have changed physically and socially. Wetherby itself has more than trebled in size in the past fifty years and some of the villages have experienced comparable expansion. Such is the pace of development, mainly of housing, that even some of the more recent scenes shown here have or are about to be changed out of all recognition.

One aspect of local life that has changed completely is transport. Apart from a few miles of track bed that have been converted to a cycleway the railway has vanished almost completely. Motor traffic in Wetherby has increased to such an extent that although the A1 bypass has been partially replaced by a new motorway, with the remainder to be upgraded to motorway standard in a few years, the town roads are frequently choked. Villages on through routes such as Boston Spa and Collingham suffer similarly.

Yet despite all these changes there are many places pictured here that are virtually unaltered so that, minus the traffic, you could stand today where the photographer stood then and imagine you had stepped back in time.

The photographs contained in this book now form part of a digital archive compiled by the Wetherby and District Historical Trust with the aim of preserving them as a record for future generations.

The crest of the Cavendish family. The 6th Duke of Devonshire, a member of the Cavendish family, sold the whole of Wetherby in the great sale of 1824.

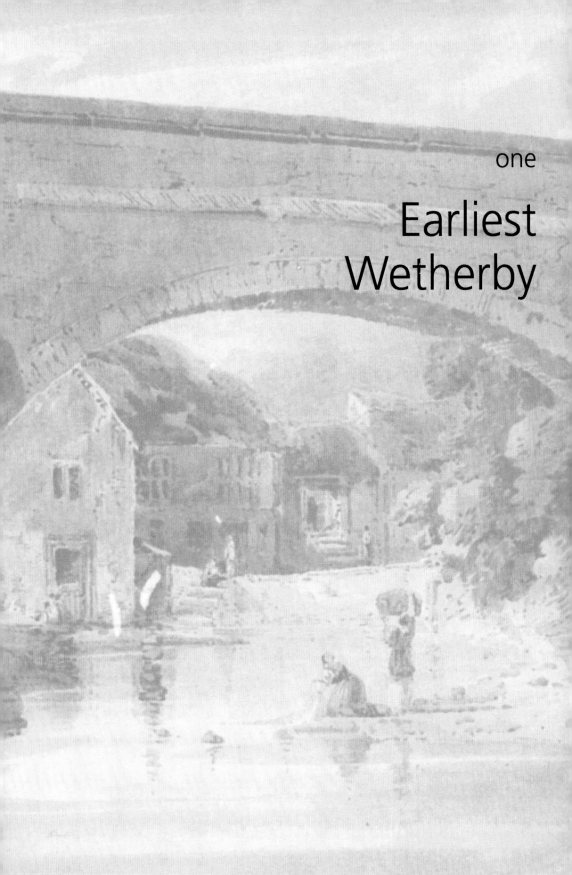

one

Earliest
Wetherby

Above and below: Our earliest records for the Wetherby area start with the Romans. In 1928 ten 'cist' graves, made with Roman roofing tiles, were found in a gravel pit next to where St James's church now stands. They also left their stone querns for grinding corn.

From Roman coins found in Wetherby, we know that they were here for a very long time. A silver coin of the Emperor Nero (A) shows his image and is hardly worn. He died in AD 68: the Romans only reached York in AD 72 and it must therefore have been lost in Wetherby soon after that date. The reverse shows the arms of a Roman legion. The Empress Sabina (B) was the wife of the Emperor Hadrian and accompanied him on his travels, almost certainly to York and perhaps to Wetherby. The reverse of this coin shows her as a goddess, so this coin was struck after she died in AD137. A coin of Constantine the Great (C) who was proclaimed emperor in York and became a Christian has on the reverse side the sun god. The letters PLN show that it was minted in London before AD 325. Emperor Theodosus appears on a coin (D) that is well worn and was struck in Yugoslavia between AD 393 and AD 395. It may have been lost here after the Romans left England in AD 410.

Above: The Saxons and Vikings only gave us our name – Wetherby – which signifies a bend in the river Wharfe. The white square on the plan shows the approximate position of a castle with its 'Sovare Keep', perhaps 100ft high with 15ft thick walls.

Above: The first bridge at Wetherby was built in 1233 through the good offices of the Archbishop of York. It was very narrow and humpback but survives as part of the present bridge. The mill and weir at Wetherby are older than the bridge; both are recorded in 1221, but like the bridge have suffered greatly through the river's flooding. This picture by the artist Girtin shows the bridge in 1800.

Right: In 1238 the Knights Templar, a crusading order, were gifted most of Wetherby and decided to move their market at Walshford to Wetherby. This is a picture of the original Market Charter granted by Henry III.

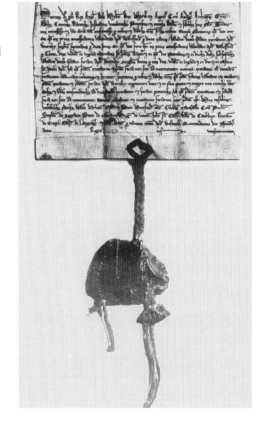

Opposite below: The site of the castle was lost until the making of a tennis court revealed the foundations. The castle was built during the Civil War in around 1140 to defend the river ford. At that time, England north of Yorkshire was held by the Scots. An 'adulterine' castle, i.e. built without royal consent, it only lasted until 1164 when Henry II had it demolished. The photograph shows a castle believed to be of similar design in Hopton, Shropshire.

PRISON

STOCKS PRISON

YORKSHIRE.

THE

Whole Town of Wetherby,

MANOR AND ESTATE OF 1300 ACRES.

Specifications

OF A CAPITAL AND EXTENSIVE

FREEHOLD ESTATE,

CONSISTING OF THE WHOLE OF

THE TOWN OF WETHERBY,

In the County of York,

Situate on the high Turnpike Road by FERRY BRIDGE to GLASGOW, distant from LEEDS 12 Miles, YORK 14, and FERRY BRIDGE 16 Miles; comprising

TWO POSTING HOUSES, THREE INNS, SEVEN PUBLIC HOUSES, EXTENSIVE WATER CORN MILLS, BREWERY, WAREHOUSES,

AND NEARLY

TWO HUNDRED DWELLING HOUSES,

WITH SEVERAL

ELIGIBLE SCITES FOR BUILDING,

On the Banks of the very beautiful River WHARFE,

Which Bounds the Estate for about One Mile and a Half.

ALSO,

The Valuable Manor of Wetherby,

COEXTENSIVE WITH THE TOWNSHIP,

With Courts Baron and Leet, Quit Rents, Toll of Fairs, the Stallage and Piccage of the Markets, Rents and Profits of the Shambles, and all other Rights, Members, and Appurtenances thereto belonging;

TOGETHER WITH

Upwards of 1300 Acres,

COMPRISING

ALL THE DESIRABLE FARMS & LANDS,

Most advantageously situate, contiguous to and entirely surrounding the Town;

THE WHOLE OF WHICH DESIRABLE PROPERTY IS IN THE OCCUPATION OF YEARLY TENANTS,
AND IS OF THE ESTIMATED VALUE OF NEARLY

Five Thousand Pounds per Annum:

Which will be Sold by Auction,

BY MESSRS. DRIVER,

Above: Wetherby existed in the parish of Spofforth with only a 'chapel of ease', built before 1546, in the middle of the Market Place. Near the chapel stood the first Town Hall, built before 1748, with prisons below for men and women and with the town stocks outside.

Left: It was in this Town Hall that in 1824 the manor of Wetherby, and almost the whole town, was sold by auction by the 6th Duke of Devonshire.

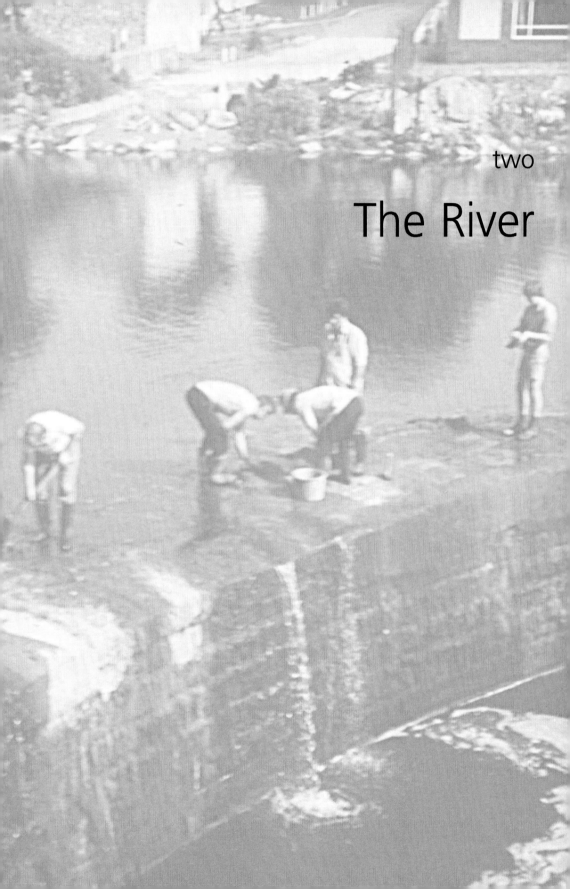

two

The River

Above: The bridge at Wetherby is the town's only 'ancient monument'. Evidence of the first three narrow arches of the original bridge can be seen incorporated under the present bridge.

Below: This view is from the south side of the weir before the salmon steps existed. The chimney is that of the gasworks built in 1845.

Wetherby Bridge & Weir, Yorkshire.

Above: The trust continues its work, and each year checks the weir for winter damage

Right: The mill fell into disuse for grinding corn, and in 1944 it burnt down whilst being used as a firelighter factory. The weir deteriorated and by 1982 was in danger of complete collapse, however, the residents of Wetherby wanted it preserved for its scenic and historical importance. The Weir Preservation Trust was formed as a charity to raise money to repair and maintain the weir, which with largely volunteer labour, was successfully done. The trust also managed to improve the whole surrounding river frontage

Close to the weir is a telegraph pole, said to be the tallest in Yorkshire, which used to take the main telegraph lines from Leeds to Tyneside. This was purchased *in situ* for one pound and fifty pence, and is now used to display the shield of Wetherby, with a weather vane above. This work was undertaken by Jack Taylor, the foreman and vice-chairman of the Weir Preservation Trust.

This millstone from the original corn mill stood at the entrance to the Old Mill dancehall, a very popular venue until it was demolished to make way for some luxury flats.

When a housing developer built the flats overlooking the weir, they found the main cog wheel from the mill. This was restored and mounted as a feature near the weir.

Following the restoration of the weir, the Lord Mayor of Leeds attended the celebration, hosted by the Town Mayor of Wetherby and chairman of the Trust.

The trust members, many of whom we see here, have also done much good work on the riverbank in the 'Wilderness' and erected seats on the side of what is now the Riverside car park.

The most recent venture of the Trust was to build a bandstand for the Wetherby Silver Band and the many visiting bands that provide much pleasure here on Sunday afternoons during the summer months. Luckily the bandstand was built to withstand flooding!

Scaur Bank playing fields have seen many functions but perhaps one of the strangest was the Evangelical Church undertaking an adult baptism in the river.

The riverbank steps also gave great pleasure to many people, mainly children, bathing. Sadly the advent of blue-green algae and other potential dangers has put an end to this practice.

The Wharfe at Wetherby was well known for its boating. Punts, rowing boats and Canadian canoes could be hired, and it was also possible to take trips on the river in a motor boat. The views of the river Wharfe are still beautiful although sadly there is no longer any boating at Wetherby.

This ruin, in the newly established Jubilee Gardens by the riverside, has now been restored and is a Grade II listed building. Its original function was as a bath house with a plunge pool below fed by very cold spring water. Above was a changing room with a warming fire. This type of building was very fashionable in Georgian times but this one now survives as a rare example.

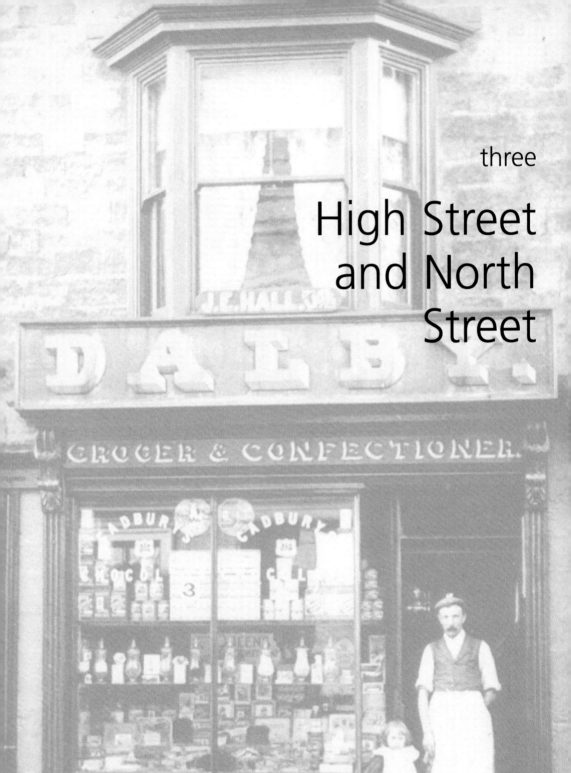

three

High Street and North Street

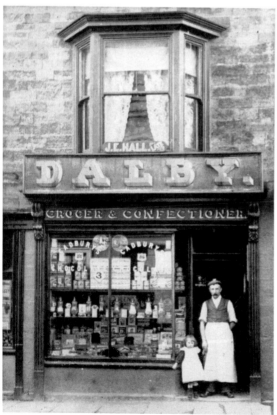

Above: The approach to the town across the River Wharfe from the Micklethwaite side of the bridge. The large building on the Wetherby side of the bridge was Bishopsgate. The absence of traffic here is surprising for a bridge which carried the Great North Road.

Left: The Dalby family were noted on both sides of the river for a variety of enterprises. One local legend has them coming across with the Normans and their name being a corruption of D'Albi.

The lower half of the High Street slopes down to the river bridge from the former New Street, now Victoria Street, on the left with Cross Street on the right. The well-remembered Hugh Hall presided over the hardware shop, second on the left. He was noted for his sharp manner in dealing with customers.

Prior to the Cattle Market being constructed in 1910, the weekly market was held in the High Street. Small temporary pens for sheep were erected and can be seen on the left. Some of the rings to which the hurdles were attached can still be seen today.

Moon's grocers shop changed owners over the years but remained a grocer's shop until the 1970s.

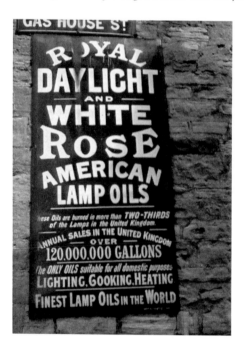

Above left: The gasworks at the end of this small side street, Gas House Street, would perhaps have had an impact on the sales of the lamp oil being advertised, but initially only a limited area would have been served by the gas street lighting which was installed in the town in 1852.

Above right: Boots were the universal footwear in both town and country - even women had their own versions to raise them above the unwelcome droppings of passing livestock. This bootmaker's shop was at the end of Victoria Street and there were a number of others around the town.

Henry Crossley not only had a virtual monopoly on the coverage of local and town news but also produced five other local papers covering an area from Otley to Tadcaster. He is described as a 'printer, publisher, and proprietor'.

The 'No Entry' sign is a reminder that traffic could emerge onto the busy High Street from the Market Place. Now only pedestrians may use this link.

This terrace of six cramped cottages on North Street, typical of old Wetherby, has now been replaced by two shops.

This scene looking up St James's Street from North Street has changed little. The buildings are largely the same but happily the road has been made up.

four

Market Place

Here are reminders of the First World War, with the gun and shell case and a striking memorial on the bridge. Today only the war memorial remains.

A substantial brewery house is the backcloth to this photograph. Workers are shown wearing clothes appropriate to their occupations. The covered wagons are reminiscent of those which opened up the prairies of North America.

A small chapel was on the site where the Town Hall now stands and the area around was still known as Chapel Hill long after the chapel ceased to exist. This side view of the Town Hall shows the tall windows of the assembly room on the first floor. A lower section to the right contained the cells, with the courtroom above, where magistrates dealt with minor crimes at their fortnightly Thursday sessions. Eventually cells were included in a new police station on Westgate, manned by an inspector and two constables. In the 1960s a new site across the river in Micklethwaite was found to erect a building to combine both the magistrates' courts and the police station.

The Town Hall and market seen shortly after the Second World War.

Above: There has been a fish and chips shop on this site for many years before other types of 'fast food' were invented. Many years ago the upstairs rooms were used as a 'doss house'.

Above: Today this gateway to the rear yard of the Three Legs public house has been incorporated into the doorway. It faces Cross Street, leading to the High Street. A cross stood at this juncture in the Market Place as a focal point for travelling preachers.

Right: This archway has now been converted into a shop window. The Thursday market continues to flourish and is host today to many more stalls than are shown here. The Black Bull, with its low roof, is one of the oldest buildings in the town.

Opposite below: The Wardman brothers carried on their family business from this shop for many years. They sold an amazing variety of items from old–fashioned tools and hardware to materials for modern DIY.

A view looking south shows the road dipping sharply to the river. Barclays Bank is a young intruder among its neighbours. The assortment of roof lines on the right is in contrast to the imposing rear wall of the Town Hall on the left.

This scene shows the north side of the Town Hall, with the roadway narrowing in the distance towards the High Street and the Angel Inn. Posts restricted vehicle access to the narrow Church Street, centre left, where craftsmen and traders lived with their families. The shop on the extreme left sold ropes made at Quarry Hill.

Striped Belisha Beacons, introduced in the 1930s, feature in this photograph. Today there are no aids to help pedestrians cross this dangerous corner. The property on the right was still mainly residential when this photograph was taken and had not yet been converted into shops.

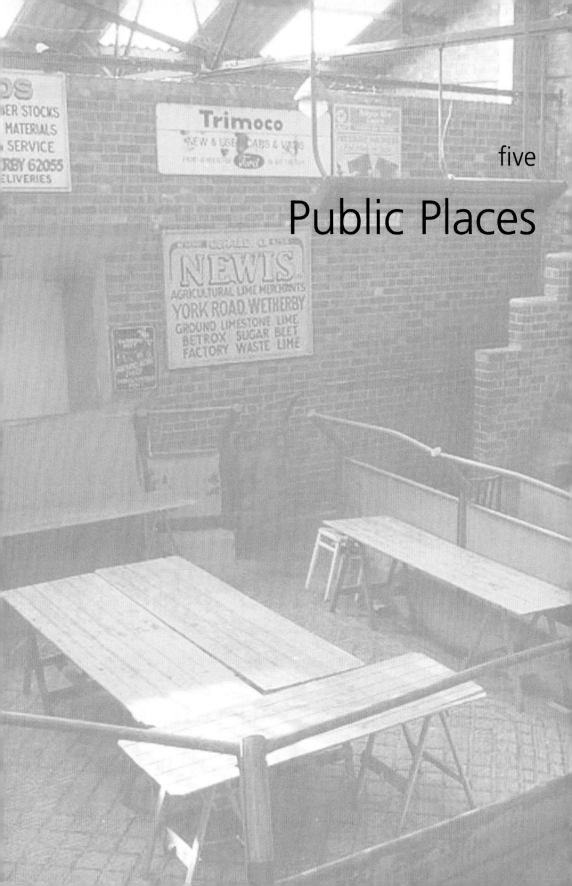

five

Public Places

The Rodney Cinema dates back to 1915, when it was known as the Raby. In middle life it operated as a bingo hall for a number of years before returning to its original function as a cinema.

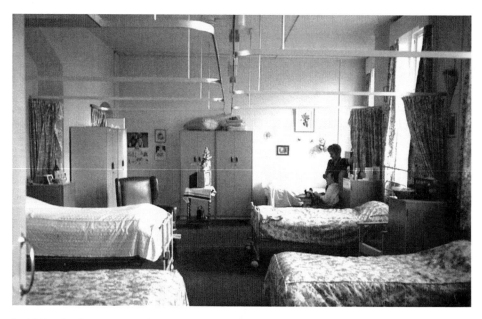

In 1863 Wharfe Grange was built as a Union Workhouse at a cost of £5,000 to cater for up to sixty inmates from Wetherby and surrounding parishes who were destitute. It was later converted into a psychiatric hospital, which closed in 1993. It has again been converted, this time into flats.

An inspector and two constables were attached to this police station in Westgate, which also had stabling for horses. Eventually a new police station was built near the roundabout, south of the town, to incorporate the magistrates' court as well as the police station.

The residents of Wetherby were understandably proud of the new Rural District Council Offices in Westgate when they were officially opened in 1938. The building included a council chamber and the administration for all services of an unusually large district area.

Although this post office building was imposing, the large area of red brick did not match any of the buildings in the market square. The upper floors were used as the sorting office and also as a telegraph and telephone exchange.

Following the demolition of the old post office, a row of small shops was built on the site. For a time the post office occupied one of these.

Eventually the post office found a home in the Co-op supermarket in the Horsefair Centre, which was later taken over by Morrison's. It did not, however, transfer to Morrison's new store and its status took a downturn.

First a temporary post office was located in the car parked behind the Catholic Church. This was far from convenient, especially when the queue extended outside on a rainy day.

The post office was briefly located at the back of this Co-op Late Shop in the Market Place, to the dismay of many residents and visitors to the town.

For many years Monday meant the livestock market in the Horsefair. A chorus of sounds from the different animals drifted over the town – accompanied by farmyard aromas!

The closeness of the market to the centre of town can be judged by this view of the animal pens, overlooked by the backs of the properties on the High street.

A moment of nostalgia is captured by local historian, Dr James Lodge, in this view of the cattle ring, which became an auction room for furniture and household goods before closure.

All signs of the livestock and market have now gone, finally a victim of the Foot and Mouth epidemic. The site is now being converted into a development of flats and shops.

In the 1920s this Garden of Rest replaced the Bowling Green Inn and a number of other small businesses, which stretched out into the middle of North Street, creating an infamous traffic bottleneck on the Great North Road, later the A1.

This house in Raby Park is only one of a succession used as Wetherby vicarages since the town became a parish in its own right instead of a township within the very large Spofforth parish.

Light manufacturing firms were located on the Sandbeck Industrial Estate, established by the Rural District Council in the 1960s to create employment locally. This aerial view is of the Farnell factory and distribution centre.

A branch of the Home Office forensic science service was located on the Industrial Estate combining laboratories previously at Harrogate and Newcastle. It was opened in 1977 by the then Home Secretary, Merlyn Rees.

The Wetherby and District Social Club was established on the estate to cater for the leisure time of the workers.

The club burned down in 2001 but has since been rebuilt.

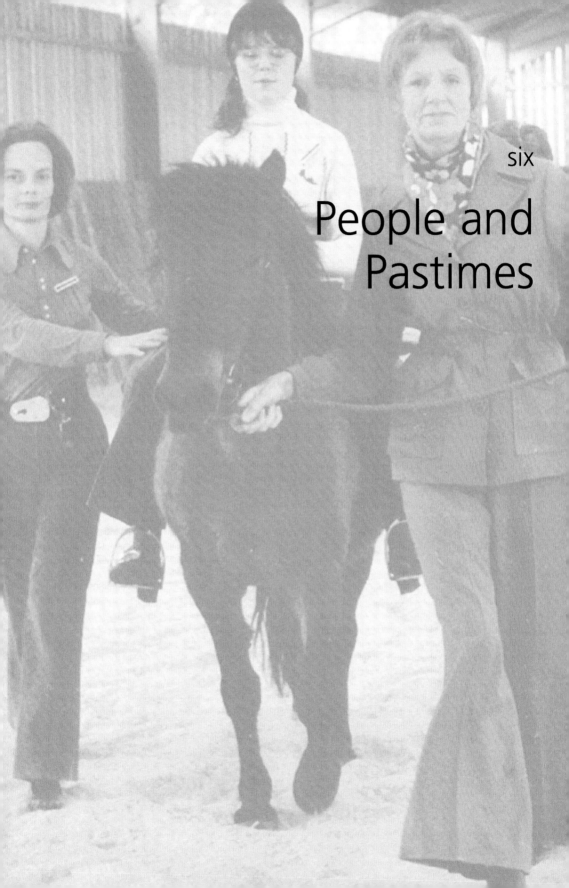

six

People and
Pastimes

Above: Quintin Rhodes (left) was a brewer who owned the Wharfedale Brewery in the Market Place. It was because of his efforts that Wetherby now has Saint James's church and the Town Hall. Revd William Raby (right) came to Wetherby in 1835 and was the last perpetual curate. He is remembered in the town by Raby Park. He wanted Wetherby to have its own church and helped Quentin Rhodes to undertake the building of St James's, built at a cost of £4,300. A day school was also started in the present Town Hall.

Left: David Hudson digging the first sod of the second bypass. Like his father, Major Hudson, he served for many years as a councillor on the Wetherby Rural District Council, Wetherby Town Council, and the West Riding Council and finally on the Leeds Metropolitan District Council. He served as Mayor of Wetherby and also Lord Mayor of the Leeds Metropolitan District.

VE day was well celebrated in 1945 by many street parties. This one is in South View, Deighton Bar. The celebrations were repeated again on the 50th anniversary.

The new Roman Catholic church was consecrated on the 11 October 1986 by the Bishop of Leeds – the Rt Revd David Konstant.

The Wetherby Saint John Ambulance Brigade, founded in the 1920s, flourished and provided first aid cover for many local events.

After the war the Air Training Corps became active in Wetherby, providing training and youth club facilities for both boys and girls.

The Boy Scouts have a long history in Wetherby, and once had the honour of the founder, Lord Baden-Powell, coming to review them outside the town hall.

The Scout camps were very popular, with the boys sleeping in tents – but do today's Scouts still encourage boxing?

Monica Dickens, the authoress and descendant of Charles Dickens, visited the local branch of Riding for the Disabled when it was formed in 1973.

A group of disabled people enjoying riding at Stockeld Park in 1999.

Town sports days were popular events in the early years of the twentieth century. The little boy in the picture is Harry Mason, who later looked after Wetherby cemetery for sixty-five years as superintendent and was awarded the MBE.

The sports days, and similar events such as the water carnival and Methodist Whitsuntide procession, led to boats, bikes, and horse-drawn carriages being gaily decorated. Those taking part were usually either in fancy dress or dressed in their finest.

Above: The bank above the Riverside car park was indeed a wilderness when Britain in Bloom started in 1989. One of their first tasks was to convert this bank into a colourful sloping garden.

Below: The object of Wetherby in Bloom was to give floral beauty to the town. This view of Bridgefoot shows that they succeeded. A pergola has now been added to the area with seating to enhance this feature at the entrance to the town.

Right: The Shambles, originally a market area for open butcher's shops, was later converted and was ideal to exhibit floral displays in a pedestrianised area.

Below: The Wetherby in Bloom team, with its many helpers, soon began to win competitions with other towns of our size. First in Yorkshire, then Britain, Europe and finally the world!

Wetherby BOSTON SPA TADCASTER & SHERBURN News

THE VOICE OF THE DISTRICT SINCE 1857   www.wetherbytoday.co.uk   Friday, September 30, 20

Our community team is the best in the world!

By Sophie Bradley

WETHERBY has seen off fierce competition from America, Canada and Japan to take top honours as one of the world's most community minded towns.

It has now been crowned the winner of an elite group of 12 towns selected by invite only to compete for the prestigious international Communities in Bloom title.

Ecstatic organisers said the win, which has praised the involvement of volunteers, businesses and councils at all levels in the community, will raise Wetherby's profile.

Chairman of Wetherby in Bloom and member of the Communities in Bloom steering committee, Geoff Humble, said it was all down to the community pulling together. "This wasn't just Wetherby in Bloom it was all the community groups. The judges grasped exactly what we were trying to do.

The steering group drove it forward but it was everyone's support which made it happen."

Mr Humble said the competition was not just about the flowers.

"It was much bigger than a normal floral competition. The trick was to pull every-

one together and we achieved that.

The judges from America and Canada stayed in Wetherby for three days with an intensive six hour judging session.

During that time they were taken to the Communities in Bloom showcase where 36 different groups had displays set up in the Methodist Chapel.

"We never thought we stood a chance," said Mr Humble.

"We were amazed and delighted to win."

Mayor of Wetherby Coun Alan Hilton said it was a great win for the town.

sophie.bradley@ypn.co.uk

World-beaters – The 'crew' of Wetherby in Bloom, pictured in the town's Garden of Rest after winning the Communities in Bloom International Competition. (2909053)

The Wetherby Arts Festival, which began in 1977, is held biennially and supports a wide range of activities, bringing many well-known artists and personalities to the town. This picture shows Barbara Windsor and the current festival chairman David Shaw.

The cast of the Wetherby Musical Theatre Group's production of *Brigadoon* in 1992.

Some members of the cast of the group's production of *Anything Goes* in 1993.

The group wanted to encourage the younger members and started The Really Youthful Musical Group, seen here in *Smike* in 1989.

Since their formation in 1966, the Wetherby Lions have done a considerable amount of work for the town, as well as raising a great deal of money for charity.

Their activities include organizing the Christmas party and 'fancy hat' competition for the old folk of the town and the annual Pram Race with teams wading the river.

Horse racing has a long tradition at Wetherby, with races taking place at a variety of sites. The present York Road course dates from 1891, with many improvements to stands, course buildings and stables taking place over the years.

MR. H. CROSSLEY (Chairman), CAPT. MONTAGU, O.B.E., M.C., J.P. (Vice-Chairman), MR. J. MELROSE, J.P. (Chairman York Race Committee), MR. C. LONG.

Some of the racecourse committee of 1921.

So popular did the race meetings become that a purpose-built railway station was erected alongside the course, which was opened in October 1924.

Special race trains, starting at Bradford, brought punters from the industrial West Riding to the race meetings.

seven

Transport

Construction of the first bypass started in 1959, shown here looking north from York Road towards Kirk Deighton.

Repairing and strengthening the bridge carrying the original bypass over the River Wharfe, weakened by forty-four years of the increasing weight of traffic.

The A1 just north of the York Road flyover showing the start of construction in 2003 of the motorway section that has replaced the road from here to Walshford as part of the upgrading of the A1 through Yorkshire.

In preparation for the upgrade of the rest of the bypass York Road flyover was itself replaced in a dramatic night-time operation in May 2004. The new bridge was moved into place by one man controlling both the huge motorised trailers with one small control box.

BRITISH RAILWAYS
NORTH EASTERN REGION

STATION GARDENS
COMPETITION
1959

FIRST CLASS
PRIZE

awarded to *Wetherby* Station

Mr. *L.W.Kean* Station Master

General Manager

Above: Wetherby passenger station, showing the main buildings. The roof of the station master's house can just be seen on the left.

Left: Between trains the staff at many small railway stations had time to produce fine garden displays. Wetherby's efforts bore fruit in 1959. Altogether it won nine 'best kept station' certificates.

A train of oil tankers passes across Wetherby golf course.

A train passes behind Northfield Place towards Wetherby goods station. A railway at the bottom of the garden must have been a delight for children but not so good for their mother's washing.

Above and below: The goods transfer shed at the original station on York Road is the only railway building still surviving in the town. Above it is seen in use, and below in its current guise as the 'The Engine Shed', an entertainment venue.

B.R. 21701

BRITISH TRANSPORT COMMISSION
BRITISH RAILWAYS

Description
Consignment **BARDSEY. N.E.R.**

From

To

Date

Train

LIVE STOCK
HANDLE WITH CARE

(This label to be used to denote that a
"Higher Value" charge has been paid on
this consignment.)

LNER 4618/7/41 20,000

LONDON & NORTH EASTERN RAILWAY.

FRAGILE LABEL
P. 3052

FRAGILE

LNER 5711/5/32 50,000

LONDON & NORTH EASTERN RAILWAY.   P 3016

Collected Luggage

From   BARDSEY. N.E.R

To _____ Station.

_____ **Railway,**

Via _____

Excess Charge to Pay _____

	No. of Pack-ages.	No. of Passengers.	
		First.	Third

Parcels stamps to be
affixed here.

FILEY

NORTH EASTERN RAILWAY.

From ___ **BARDSEY. N.E.R**

Above: The railway touched all aspects of daily life. Every station, no matter how small, handled a very wide range of items from luggage to livestock and passengers to parcels.

Below: A local freight train is about to cross the bridge near the Masonic Hall in Deighton Road. The advertisements for cars and vans reflect the increase in motor transport, which sounded the death knell for many local branch lines including the ones that served the town.

This transport café stood opposite the Masonic Hall and was very well used when the A1 ran through the town. When the bypass opened trade declined considerably, leading to its closure within a few years.

With hindsight it is ironic to see the railway being demolished just as the town was expanding rapidly. The house prices advertised seem unbelievable now but were from three to five times the average yearly wage at the time.

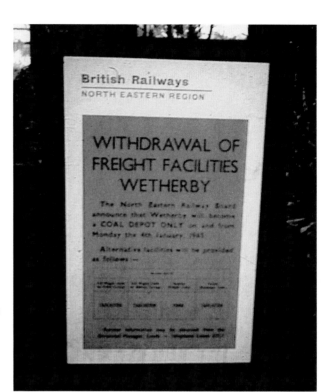

Right: With the passenger service withdrawn, the freight service only lasted until January 1965 before that too was withdrawn.

Below: The very last train to leave Wetherby was a photo opportunity for one young girl in 1966.

The track was soon taken up and sent for recycling.

With the track and station buildings gone the signal box and water pump were next in line for demolition. The station site is now a car park and an entry point for the Harland Way.

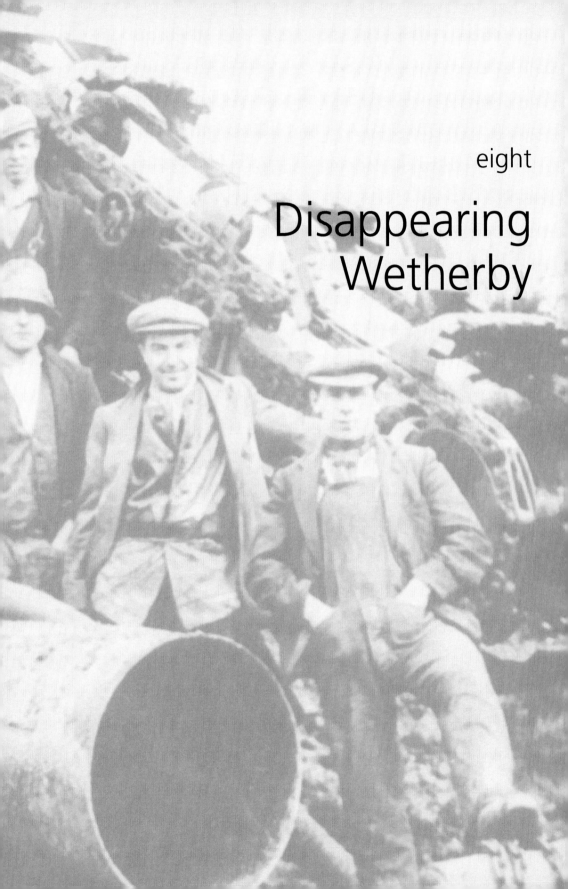

eight

Disappearing Wetherby

Wetherby had always been a rural market town. This was Hill Top farm on Spofforth hill, owned by the Hudson family. It is now a large housing estate. The boy in the picture is David Hudson, who later became the Mayor of Wetherby and Lord Mayor of Leeds.

An idyllic view of the same farm: the men are hay turning. The advent of the tractor, and other mechanized farm machinery, has so reduced the required manpower that very few people now work on the land.

Looking north towards Kirk Deighton in the early 1970s. The nearer fields are now part of the 'Rivers' housing estate the result of the population growing from 4,179 in 1961 to 10,077 in 1978, and it's still growing!

Sandbeck Garage on the Deighton Road. The field to the right was part of Skirrows Farm, and is now part of the Sandbeck Industrial estate.

The crew of HMS *Ceres* parade on their quarterdeck. Hostels built in wartime for munitions workers at Thorpe Arch were taken over by the Royal Navy in 1942, first as HMS *Cabot*, which the Germans claimed to have sunk(!), then as HMS *Demetrius*, and finally as HMS *Ceres* until its closure in 1958. The prison service took over the camp as a Borstal, then a Youth Custody Centre and now a Youth Offenders Institution.

The first four nuns came to Wetherby in 1932 to start a convent in Barleyfields Road, and as a teaching order also set up Saint Philomenas School which in 1969 became Saint Joseph's Catholic aided state school. The two nuns are seen wearing their distinctive habits. Sister Theresa, the senior nun, is on the left. The nuns have now left Wetherby.

The York Road-Deighton Road junction looking northwest towards the late Miss Robinson's house, in ruins. The site is now occupied by the York Road flats, at first nicknamed Hodgson's horrors. Mabel Hodgson was a district counsellor who strongly opposed the building of these flats, but after the first development a further block was erected and named Hodgson House!

This site on the west side of North Street has had a series of garages on it, with different owners and designs which changed dramatically over the years.

Inside the workshops of Teasdale & Metcalfe, once the largest employer in Wetherby. Their barns and steel-framed buildings can still be seen all over Britain together with their distinctive logo.

The junction of Horsefair and Hallfield Lane with the Cattle Market on the left. The site on the right had been Teasdale and Metcalfe's and would soon be the Co-op supermarket - now Morrison's.

Right: This one-up, one-down house was on the north side of the Horsefair where Morrison's now have their goods yard.

Below: This block of brick houses stood facing the Cattle Market at the junction of Hallfield Lane and Walton road. It was always known as of the 'Cluster of Nuts'. Each house had a coal cellar - but no bathroom.

This large house decorated for King George's Silver Jubilee, on the north side of Crossley Street, was built soon after the First World War as a boy's club and then became the first offices of the Wetherby Rural District Council. The site is now occupied by the Crossley Street Surgery.

The house of Hick the chimney sweep on Westgate was demolished to form the entrance for the new council offices in 1937.

The Rendezvous café was on the left as you entered the Market Place from the bridge. In turn it had been a Wimpey burger café, bookshop, and carpet shop, before becoming a café again. This has now been demolished and there is a restaurant here in an new building.

This lane now leads to the swimming pool and the new sports facilities on the Ings. There was no swimming pool when this photograph was taken, but there was a very smelly piggery.

Sewage disposal was always a problem for the town. These men are laying the pipes for the original sewage works on the Ings.

A very large group of Wesleyan Methodists on the platform of the passenger station. Slater Whitfield and his wife memorably celebrated their golden wedding by taking their friends, and the Chapel Sunday School and choir, for a day's outing to Scarborough.

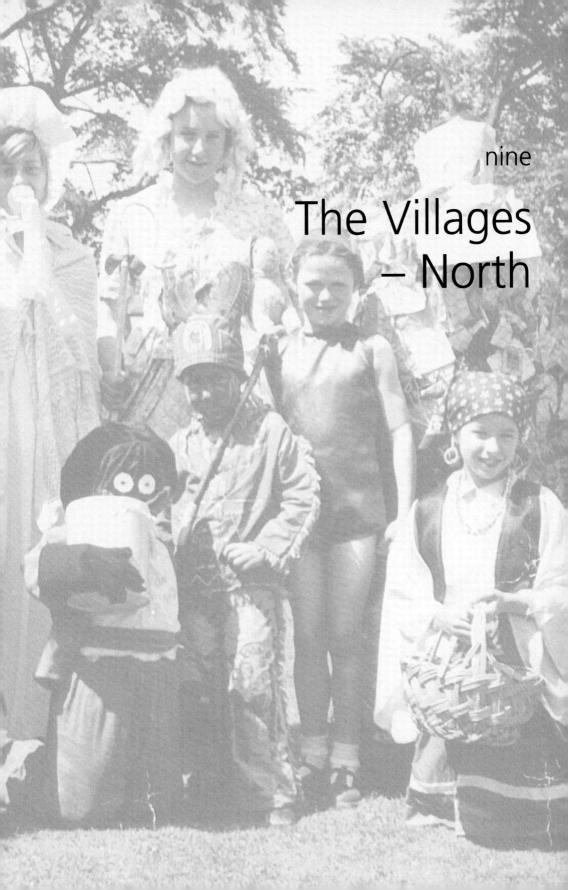

nine

The Villages
– North

Little Ribston

Ribston Hall was built in 1674. Attached to the hall on the right is the church of St Andrews, Great Ribston, built in the thirteenth century for the Knights Templar.

The Dents of Ribston were a wealthy and important family, occupying the hall from 1835. This is the family carriage waiting to take the master to Wetherby railway station.

The main road through Little Ribston has hardly changed although the traffic is busier today.

The village had a post office – but like so many others this has now closed.

The village chapel has survived. Originally a carpenters shop, it was bought by the Dents who then added the western porch so there was a place of worship in the village without the need to walk to the hall.

This stone marks the last part of the forest of Knaresborough to be enclosed in 1778. King John is reputed to have frequently hunted there.

Hunsingore

Above: This mill on the River Nidd at Hunsingore is now a private house. The river downstream of this point was one of the most popular in the region for otter hunting.

Right: Hunsingore has not only lost its mill but the village school and the post office as well.

Cowthorpe

Cowthorpe was known for its famous old oak tree, said to be over a thousand years old. Sadly it is no more: however, a new tree has been planted in its place, grown from an acorn from the original tree.

The village pub was called the Old Oak and catered for anglers on the nearby river, of which it owned four miles of excellent fishing rights. Fishing was illegal on Sundays so the pub only had a six-day licence.

Kirk Deighton

Near the Church is the Kirk Deighton Manor house, built as a rectory before 1840 by James Geldart who, as patron, presented himself to the living in 1795. He was followed as rector by his son and then his grandson, who died in 1914; they each employed a curate.

The view of Kirk Deighton Main Street has changed little over the years except that there were two pubs side by side. The Greyhound has now gone, incorporated into the Bay Horse.

Above: The approach to the church is also little altered except the houses are no longer thatched. The road has been widened and the church now has gates.

Left: Have you ever wondered how a church steeple is repaired? This is how it was done in Kirk Deighton before the days of Health and Safety rules.

The church school was opposite the church and the headmistress lived in the tied house to the left in the picture. Now both are private houses.

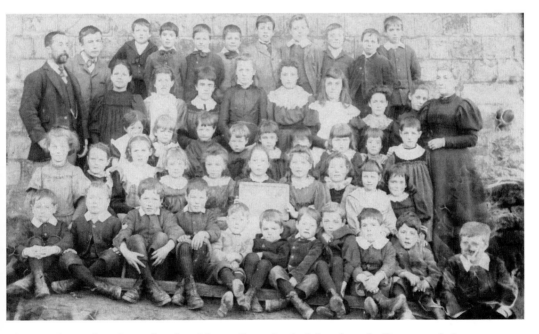

These are the pupils at the small Kirk Deighton village school, all from large families, most of whose parents worked on the local farms.

The farm workers' houses were built of stone, near the road but with long gardens behind to grow food for the family.

Here is Mr Featherstone of Kirk Deighton standing beside a West Riding County Council steam lorry, number WR6377.

During the Second World War purpose-built huts were erected as living accommodation for the Land Army girls working on local farms. These are Land Army girls from the First World War who were usually billeted at the farms.

Many villages still hold an annual fête or show with fancy dress competitions. This is a post-war competition held in Kirk Deighton which obviously gave great pleasure to these children and parents alike.

VE day was one of great rejoicing throughout the country, with many street parties. This photograph shows one such party held on open land at South View, Deighton Bar, an area now filled with houses and considered part of Wetherby.

At one time there were six toll bar houses in the Wetherby area. This is the only one remaining, built in 1784 at the junction of the old Great North Road and the Knaresborough Road. This one had toll gates across both roads to collect the charges.

ten

The Villages
– South

Bardsey

A view from the Bingley Arms in the old village of Bardsey, reputedly the oldest inn in England. A truly rural view.

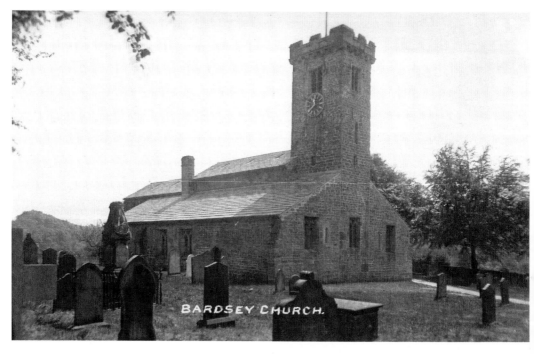

BARDSEY CHURCH.

The Church of All Hallows with its Saxon tower, to which narrow Norman aisles were added, looks at peace with the world. William Congreve, the dramatist, was baptized here in 1669.

COUNTY COUNCIL OF THE WEST RIDING OF YORKSHIRE

EDUCATION COMMITTEE

The Chairman and Members of the Wetherby District Sub-Committee
and the Headmistress of the School request the pleasure of your
company on the occasion of the formal opening of

BARDSEY PRIMARY SCHOOL

by

HER ROYAL HIGHNESS THE PRINCESS ROYAL

on MONDAY, 9th APRIL, 1951, at 2-15 p.m.

All guests must be in their places by 2-0 p.m.

Please reply to
The Headmistress

THIS CARD ADMITS
ONE PERSON

The old Bardsey school was situated in the now renamed Callister Memorial Hall. The new school
was opened in 1951 by Alice, the Princess Royal.

A report in an architectural magazine described the new school as 'interesting modern buildings,
nicely grouped on a gentle incline'. For the children it was light and airy with much more room.

The view looking down on the main Leeds to Wetherby road with the railway line and the station, built in 1900 and closed in 1966. Today the embankment has been removed and houses are on both sides of the road and the station site.

Once closed, demolition quickly followed. This bridge has also gone. It once led to Bardsey Mill, which was owned for many years by the Mawson family and provided animal feeds and seed for the local farms.

This view of the village street can still be recognized but the village shop, telephone box, and post office have all gone.

G. H. MOON & SON
FAMILY GROCERS
EAST KESWICK

WINE & SPIRIT
MERCHANTS

Tel. Collingham Bridge 473.

TO THE MOST IMPORTANT PERSON IN OUR BUSINESS

We have pleasure in sending you our latest price list, which offers a wide selection of goods at competive prices.

May we respectfully offer our services, and invite you to call and view our stock, or send your order by post or phone when it will receive our prompt and careful attention.

Thanking you for your valued support, and looking forward to the pleasure of attending to your requirements for the coming season.

We remain,
Yours faithfully,
G. H. MOON & SON
Ltd.

Moon and Son, grocers, had other branches in the area but this wine and spirit merchant also relied on trade from outside the village of East Keswick.

A view down the village street before 1910 with an unmade road, thatched cottage and the village pump.

Progress is seen here as the road is now made up, a hedge at Low Cottage has replaced the fence and the telephone service has reached the village. Today, would the planners allow the thatched cottage to be demolished, or to erect a wooden hut as a shop?

The Travellers Rest coaching inn on the Harewood Avenue, turnpike under an Act of 1753, and with a lovely view over the Wharfe valley to Woodhall and the distant Almscliffe Crag.

The same building in more modern times. Recently, after a major fire, it has changed again.

The unmade-up road of Harewood Avenue joins the Leeds to Wetherby road in the centre of Collingham with an old version of the Half Moon Inn on the left. The elaborate stonework of the wall remains unchanged today.

The Old Star Inn building is largely unchanged, although the entrance is different, as is the type of transport for visitors. The adjoining building was a barn but is now part of the inn.

The mill and pond at Collingham have gone but the building remains.

Collingham is not mentioned in Domesday Book but this old church contains some Saxon crosses, the most interesting in the area.

The stepping stones remain today across the beck on the walk to the river.

The railway bridge over the river Wharfe between Collingham and Linton fell to the Beeching axe. All that is left today are the concrete bases on the river bed.

The first railway line through Collingham was single track and opened in 1876, but the railways were labour intensive and this village station was employing six men by 1910.

A view looking from the bridge over the Harewood road at Collingham station. There were two main lines and several sidings. The trains stacked here were waiting to take the crowds home from the Wetherby races. The royal family used Collingham station when they visited the Princess Royal at Harewood House.

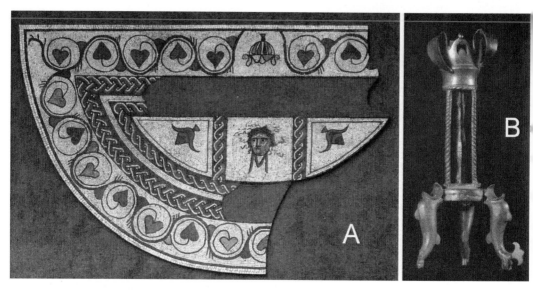

Near Collingham, at Compton, ploughing revealed Roman remains in 1845. The Victorians were delighted to unearth this lovely mosaic of Medusa (A). Archeological techniques had improved by the 1980s and a full scientific excavation of the area revealed an Iron Age settlement, Roman villa, and Saxon burials. One of the finds was this fine copper candlestick (B).

The Boston cross roads are in the parish of Collingham, but who would recognize this scene today? The A1 was still a single track road, though work had already started to make it a dual carriageway and change the crossroads to an underpass.

Boston Spa

On the road from the crossroads to the village of Boston Spa stood a toll-bar house. This was the main Otley to Tadcaster road. The vehicle with the barrel on top was used for watering the road to keep the dust down.

This hotel was one of the first large buildings to be built in Boston Spa. It was built to serve those who came 'to take the waters'. Its name was later changed to The Royal, but it is no longer an inn and has been converted to flats and shops.

A view of the main streets of Boston Spa with a bus of the time. Sefton café was very popular and remained for a long time.

A spring accidentally discovered on the riverbank in 1744 led to the birth of the spa and this fine building on the site. Boston Spa aspired to rival Harrogate. That hope was never fulfilled but it did become a very scenic village.

Opposite below: Motor transport put the village back on the map with the establishment of a regular bus service to the cities.

Above: One of the factors against the development of the spa was the lack of a railway station in the village. Visitors had to be collected by carriage from Thorp Arch station.

The village soon developed shops for the upper classes, like this off-licence, not common at that time. This one also specialized in cocoa, chocolates, beer and brandy.

Village shops bedecked with advertisements at a time when cycling was fashionable. Note the National Provincial & Union Bank of England - a small branch site!

Bramham

Bramham Village.

The road from Thorner passes down Tenter Hill to meet the Great North Road in the centre of Bramham, in an age without motor cars Eventually something had to be done for the motor car and the A1 that passed through the centre of the village was rerouted on a bypass in the early 1960s: the village then escaped the constant danger and sound of traffic.

Bramham village square with an impressive war memorial and a village pump with two spouts – one for human consumption and one for the use of wagons and animals.

Left: All Saints church has a Norman tower and a steeple which was once damaged by lightning. It would appear the haystack in the church yard escaped.

Below: Bramham College, a very upmarket boys school, was opened in 1842 and survived until a severe outbreak of cholera in 1869 killed a number of the pupils. After laying derelict for a number of years the building was demolished and the stone used to rebuild Bramham Park House in 1907. Bramham Park, now the home of the Lane-Fox family, was originally built by the first Lord Bingley in 1710. He was a self-made man, Lord Mayor and MP for York, and a favourite of Queen Anne. The park now hosts the well-known Bramham Horse Trials and the Leeds Music Festival each year.

Clifford

In the background of this view looking down Clifford main street can be seen the large Roman Catholic church of Saint Edward, opened in 1848. Many Roman Catholics came to Clifford from Ireland to work in the large flax mill in the village.

This view looks up Clifford main street, 1910. The village was struck by poverty when the flax mill burned down in 1867 and the industry died. The shop on the left of the picture can be seen in more detail over the page.

A grocers and draper's shop on the corner of Clifford Street with the staff of five posing for a photograph. The shop also acted as the village post office according to the sign above the door. The appearance of this shop has changed very little even today.

Clifford convent was founded in 1851 by the Sisters of Mercy, a teaching order, who ran a primary school. In 1892 they added a girls' boarding school. The building has now been demolished and the site is part of a housing development.

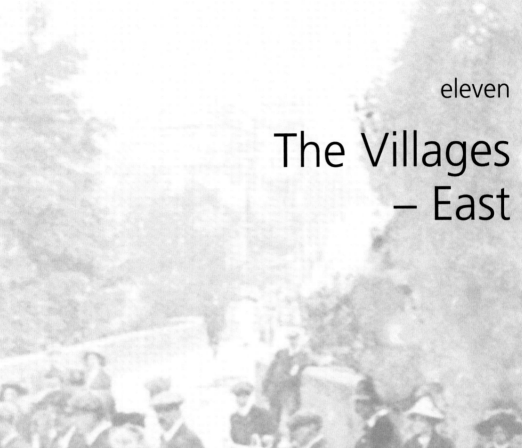

eleven

The Villages – East

THORPARCH
Coronation Festivities
IN CONNECTION WITH THE
CORONATION OF KING GEORGE V.
ON THURSDAY, JUNE 22nd, 1911.

COMMITTEE.
Chairman—T. B. MATTHEWS, Esq.
Vice—Mrs. MATTHEWS.

Rev. H. W. Griffith.
Mr. C. Richardson.
Mr. R. Scollick.
Mr. W. Mortimer.
Mr. J. Spenceley.
Mr. W. Hatfield.
Mr. T. Gaines.
Mr. R. Whitcup.

Mr. W. Fisher.
Mr. W. Wilson.
Mr. W. Wharton.
Mr. G. Blenden.
Mr. W. Hawe.
Mr. C. Jameson.
Mr. J. Standidge.
Mr. W. Battery.

Mr. J. SIMPSON, Hon. Secretary.

PROGRAMME FOR THE DAY.

Procession from Village Green to Church, 10-45 a.m.
Coronation Service in Church, 11 a.m.
Cricket Match, 1 p.m.   Children's Sports, 2 p.m.
Tea for the Children in the Park, 3 & 3-30.   Tea for Adults, 4-30.
Dancing, 7 o'clock.

"GOD SAVE THE KING."
[OVER.

Left: The village of Thorp Arch was considerably smaller in 1910 than it is today but they made sure their festivities for the coronation of George V would be first rate. From the program we can see that they needed a committee of twenty-two to organize it!

Below: The entrance to Thorp Arch Hall in about 1910, when children could safely play in the middle of the road.

Thorp Arch

The Bramham Moor foxhunt met twenty times a year near Boston Spa, but this meet, photographed on the Thorp Arch end of the Boston Bridge in 1912, is the local otter hunt. Records show that the lady with the bike is the district nurse!

This meet of hounds on Thorp Arch green is the beagle hunt. They hunted on foot and chased hares.

A lovely view from Thorp Arch bridge of the weir and mill. The latter made cotton bobbins. Note the horse and cart collecting gravel from the shingle bed.

In the old days it was a sleepy village, as the man leaning on the wall outside the Pax Inn suggests. The inn lost its thatch and was later rebuilt and the village is now far from sleepy.

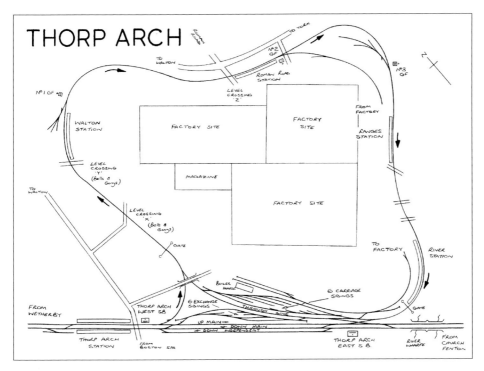

THORP ARCH

(map labels:) TO YORK · N°2 GF · TO WALTON · ROMAN ROAD STATION · N°3 GF · LEVEL CROSSING 'Z' · FROM FACTORY · N°1 GF · FACTORY SITE · FACTORY SITE · RANGES STATION · WALTON STATION · LEVEL CROSSING 'Y' (Bells & Gongs) · MAGAZINE · TO WALTON · LEVEL CROSSING 'X' (Bells & Gongs) · FACTORY SITE · GATE · TO FACTORY · RIVER STATION · BOILER HOUSE · 6 CARRIAGE SIDINGS · FROM WETHERBY · THORP ARCH WEST SB · 6 EXCHANGE SIDINGS · THROUGH LINE · GATE · UP MAIN · DOWN MAIN · DOWN INDEPENDENT · THORP ARCH STATION · FROM BOSTON SPA · THORP ARCH EAST S.B. · RIVER WHARFE · FROM CHURCH FENTON

In 1942 this area, and particularly this village, saw enormous changes following the opening of a major ordnance factory with its own railway connection to the national railway system. The site is now occupied by an industrial estate, the National Lending Library and shopping areas. There is also now a large prison and remand centre on part of the site.

The munitions factory was next to the public road to Wighill separated only by a wire fence between. Luckily there were never any serious accidents.

Left: The factory produced all types of ordnance, bombs, torpedoes, shells and small arms ammunition. Here are some of the enormous bombs built on the site, which employed a vast number of (mainly female) workers.

Below: The railway system was vital to the factory, not only to carry a constant supply of these huge bombs and the other ordnance safely to the military, but also to bring the assembly workers here by special trains from as far away as Hull. Having been built to cover a wartime emergency the factory surprisingly survived until 1958.

Walton

The factory had little impact on the village of Walton although it was partially in the parish. Post-war building and the industrial estate has made an even larger impact on life here.

The village main street in about 1910. The Fox Inn is on the left.

Wighill

A typical thatched agricultural worker's cottage in 1904. Such cottages would have had no piped water, sewage disposal or electricity.

The Bramham Moor Hunt and foxhounds outside the White Swan.

An aerial view of the centre of the village in 1966. At this time it was very much still a farming village but now many of the farm buildings have been made into private houses.

This assembled group of inhabitants, photographed in about 1900, may be the total population of the village. Unfortunately the occasion for the photograph was not recorded.

Bilton in Ainsty

The centre of the village of Bilton as it was in 1904 shows a quiet and peaceful place. It retains its quiet aspect even today.

The late Norman church of St Helen's stands distant from the old village but near the main road. It has changed little over the centuries.

twelve

The Villages
– West

Spofforth

Always known as Spofforth Castle, this building is in fact a fortified manor house, begun after 1308 as the home of the Percy family. In 1309 the family bought Alnwick castle which then became their principal home.

This road junction now has a roundabout and the garage site has been redeveloped with houses.

Follifoot Road before the village's Long Memorial Hall was built.

Above: Spofforth railway station looking towards
Wetherby. The level crossing is on the Wetherby
Road, and near the Railway Inn, today far from
any trains. When the railway from Church Fenton
to Harrogate was being built it reached Spofforth
in 1847 and stopped here. The railway construction
workers were billeted in the village and when a
manager absconded with their pay, they rioted. The
last four and a half miles to Harrogate had to wait
another year to open while a tunnel and viaduct
were built.

Right: A ticket collector at Spofforth station wearing
the uniform of the North Eastern Railway (NER).

Council houses off the Follifoot road, built to a very unusual design.

This large house, just outside Spofforth, was built as the Dower House for the Middleton family of Stockeld. Later it became a Quaker refuge for battered women, then a Cheshire Home and now it is converted for private housing.

Sicklinghall

Looking up the main street of Sicklinghall with the Scotts Arms on the right. This view is little changed today but the unmade road tells of another age.

This is the opposite view looking down the hill. The village has of course now lost its post office!

Sicklinghall has long been influenced by the Roman Catholic centre at Stockeld and this small village still has a Catholic church. There was also a recovery centre for priests and the convent shown here in this photograph.

Strangely the late Georgian house called Wood Hall is in the parish of Sicklinghall although its drive leads to Linton. A mansion built for a gentleman, it became a boys' boarding school. The headmaster, Jack Catlow, had been tutor to the German President Hindenberg. After closure as a school, the hall became an ecumenical centre and is now an hotel.

Linton was once a small village surrounded by countryside.

A quiet scene in the village looking towards Wetherby. Most of these houses are still there but this is the Linton of 100 years ago.

Other local titles published by The History Press

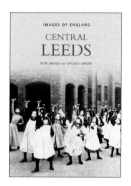

Central Leeds

ROSE GIBSON

This impressive selection of over 200 old photographs and illustrations whisks the reader away on an exciting and informative tour of central Leeds as it used to be. Spanning well over 100 years, these images – drawn primarily from Leeds Central Library's extensive photo archive and now made available on the 'Leodis' website (www.leodis.net) – provide a revealing insight into the past as they bring the old city to life.

0 7524 4005 5

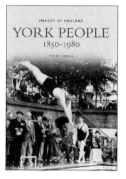

York People

YVETTE TURNBULL

Compiled from York Libraries and Archives' photographic website Imagine York, this absorbing collection offers a glimpse into the lives of some of the people who shaped the history and character of this great city in the nineteenth and twentieth centuries. Images range from those of people laughing at a gala or enjoying a day out at the races to pictures of families fighting to make the best of life in the face of adversity. There is something here for anyone who has an interest in the city of York and would like to know more about its history.

0 7524 3716 X

Haunted Leeds

KEN GOOR

From creepy accounts of the city centre to phantoms of the theatre, inns and hotels, *Haunted Leeds* contains a chilling range of ghostly phenomena. Drawing on historical and contemporary sources, you will hear about the Leeds Witch, the Beastie of Butts Corner, a former librarian who haunts the Leeds Library, the ghost of Bond Street shopping centre and many more ghostly goings-on.

0 7524 4016 0

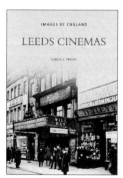

Leeds Cinemas

ROBERT E. PREEDY

Through the medium of old photographs, programmes and advertisements, this book provides a fascinating look at the history of cinema-going in the city of Leeds and its suburbs over the last hundred years. Including chapters on technology, entrepreneurs and cinema chains, *Leeds Cinemas* will delight all those who have fond memories of visiting some of Leeds' picture houses, many of which have now disappeared, as well as anyone interested in the architectural and social history of the city.

0 7524 3583 3

If you are interested in purchasing other books published by The History Press, or in case you have difficulty finding any of our books in your local bookshop, you can also place orders directly through our website
www.thehistorypress.co.uk

IMAGES OF ENGLAND

WETHERBY
AND SURROUNDING
VILLAGES

Wetherby

Historical Trust